Learning Differences
in the
Classroom

Elizabeth N. Fielding
The Meadowbrook School
Weston, Massachusetts, USA

International Reading Association
800 Barksdale Road, PO Box 8139
Newark, Delaware 19714-8139, USA
www.reading.org

The International Reading Association attempts, through its publications, to provide a forum for a wide spectrum of opinions on reading. This policy permits divergent viewpoints without implying the endorsement of the Association.

Director of Publications   Joan M. Irwin
Assistant Director of Publications   Jeanette K. Moss
Senior Editor   Matthew W. Baker
Assistant Editor   Janet S. Parrack
Assistant Editor   Tori Mello
Publications Coordinator   Beth Doughty
Association Editor   David K. Roberts
Production Department Manager   Iona Sauscermen
Art Director   Boni Nash
Electronic Publishing Supervisor   Wendy A. Mazur
Electronic Publishing Specialist   Anette Schütz-Ruff
Electronic Publishing Specialist   Cheryl J. Strum
Electronic Publishing Assistant   Peggy Mason

Library of Congress Cataloging in Publication Data
Fielding, Elizabeth N.
    Learning differences in the classroom/Elizabeth N. Fielding.
        p.   cm.
    Includes bibliographical references.
    1. Learning disabled children—Education—United States.
2. Cognitive styles in children—United States.   I. Title.
LC4705.F54   1999   99-22994
371.92'6—dc21
ISBN 0-87207-251-7

◆◆◆

dedicated to Chris

Introduction

Every child is unique. Each brings to the classroom a set of experiences, knowledge, and motivations that is like no other child's. Although every individual has a style of learning that is most comfortable and facilitative for them, some children also have learning differences that make classroom learning particularly difficult. These children face daily challenges in the classroom that are separate from their innate ability, their motivation, and their effort. Sometimes these differences are severe enough to be termed *learning disabilities*, but often they are subtle and compensated for, so that children rely on their own intelligence, perseverance, and strategies to function in the classroom. A teacher can play a critical role in recognizing and understanding these learning differences. In fact, one teacher's understanding of a child's learning differences and challenges can change that child's entire academic life.

This booklet will focus on five different areas of potential learning difficulties: auditory processing, visual processing, organizational skills, attention deficits, and written output difficulties. Each section provides a description of the difficulty and the role it plays in classroom learning, then offers strategies for helping children with the difficulty in the classroom.

◆

One teacher's understanding of a child's learning differences and challenges can change that child's entire academic life.

◆

These five areas were selected because they are often overlooked in the classroom due to their subtlety. Diagnosis of difficulty in these areas is at times complicated, and many evaluators do not systematically include all five of these areas as part of a testing battery. Yet, these areas affect virtually all other academic subjects in the classroom. It is important for both the teacher and the student to understand the student's learning strengths and weaknesses in order for the student to be successful in the current year and beyond.

The intent of this booklet is to help teachers to recognize, understand, and work with these subtle learning differences. The suggestions included are by no means inclusive, but are ones that I have used successfully with like children. The information presented is suggested as a guide for teachers as they strategize to meet the needs of their individual students. Although no two children learn in the same way, some children do have significant learning difficulties; thus teachers may need to enlist the help of specialized professionals for determining whether a specific learning disability is present in a student. In addition, many readers might want to further the information given in this booklet by reading related research journals or academic texts (see Appendix B on page 27 for a list of suggested readings). It is hoped that this text will open a door to dialogue and discussion among teachers and with teachers and their students.

The text also is designed to serve as a resource for teachers in working with parents, because most parents do not have a background in learning issues. The material in this booklet can help parents come to understand their child's learning both at school and at home.

Auditory Processing

Devon sits in the front of the classroom, but is distracted constantly. "What page did you say? I didn't hear you," is often heard from her. If you don't answer her requests, she becomes quite anxious and agitated. It seems that virtually every time new or complex information is presented, you need to sit down with her and explain it to her individually. Unfortunately, although you would like to be able to do this, you have many other children in your classroom that need you, too.

Devon's behaviors are typical of a child who has *auditory processing problems*. Auditory processing problems occur when a child has difficulty processing the meaning of language. These children often have normal hearing acuity, but it is in the *understanding* of what is being said with which they have difficulty (Singer, 1991). In the classroom, these children may display a variety of behaviors:

◆ Difficulty understanding or remembering what has been said

◆ Inability to carry out multistep oral directions correctly

◆ Mixing up similar sounding words

◆ Distractibility or daydreaming while listening

◆ Needing extra time to process auditory information, such as questions

◆ Poor phonetic skills

How do I know if a child has an auditory processing problem?

Although auditory processing might appear to be a basic, observable trait, weaknesses in this area often go undiagnosed or are misdiagnosed. It can be difficult to determine whether anxious, distractible, inattentive behavior is due to auditory problems, attentional problems, emotional problems, or something else entirely. Therefore, a screening by a trained audiologist (either in a hospital setting or privately) is the best way to determine if there is an auditory weakness. This type of screening usually includes various headphone listening tasks that measure the child's listening and processing skills. This testing can indicate where the difficulty lies: in language processing, speed of processing, word discrimination, memory, sequencing, or elsewhere. A screening also will give an indication of what percentage of correct processing a child has in each ear, for instance 33% accuracy for left ear and 80% accuracy for right ear.

What strategies can I use in the classroom?

There are several steps a teacher can take to help a student with auditory challenges in the classroom:

1. *Provide preferential seating.* Generally speaking, the best place to seat students with auditory difficulties is close to the teacher and near the chalkboard. This helps keep them "tuned in" and free from distraction, and they can receive the visual reinforcement of the chalkboard.

2. *Speak into the "good" ear.* When working with students, try to sit on the side of their "good" ear. As mentioned above, a screening report will indicate the percentage of successful processing for each ear. If a screening report is unavailable, sit to the child's right side. Because of the way the brain is typically organized with the language processing areas located in the left hemisphere (Healy, 1994), the right ear is generally the stronger ear for processing. This can be particularly true for children with difficulties.

3. *Offer visual reinforcement of oral information.* Reinforce oral directions by writing key points on the chalkboard. Outlines, assignments, page numbers, and multistep directions all can be written down, and will supply visual reinforcement for these students. In addition, have students keep a homework record book that you check daily. This will allow you to see what the student has written down *before* the assignment is done.

4. *Optimize the strengths.* When testing, give the student an opportunity to capitalize on her strengths. If the student is highly visual, a diorama, poster, or oral presentation in English, history, or science may be easier and may show her potential more adequately than requiring a written report or standard pencil and paper test.

◆

Generally speaking, the best place to seat students with auditory difficulties is close to the teacher and near the chalkboard.

◆

5. *Help the student focus.* A gentle touch on the shoulder or even just gravitating toward the student's desk can bring an unfocused student back into focus. It is particularly essential to make sure the student is focused on you when announcing important information, such as assignments.

6. *Have the student repeat information.* If you have given lengthy or complex assignments, have the student repeat back to you privately what you have said in order to check that she has all information correct.

7. *Repeat yourself when necessary.* Be willing to repeat information. Children with auditory processing problems cannot function in an "I will only say this once" type of classroom. Understandably, repeating information can be frustrating for the teacher. However, as the teacher comes to understand and compensate for this type of learning style, information should have to be repeated less often.

8. *Speak slowly*. The faster a teacher speaks, the quicker she will "lose" students who have auditory processing problems. Be aware of how fast you speak. Often slowing the rate of normal speech can help students with listening difficulties tremendously.

9. *Reduce noise levels*. Be conscious of the level of noise in the classroom, particularly when you are speaking. Some children can process adequately in a quiet environment, but have extreme difficulty when they are in noisy environments. Try to avoid giving assignments or important announcements when children are moving around the classroom or going to lunch or recess.

10. *Allow extra time*. For many students, their first reaction is to ask "What?" when complex information has been presented. Before you answer, allow some extra time for processing. Often, this is all they need. At the same time, when you ask students questions, give them ample time before expecting an answer or assuming they do not know an answer.

11. *Help students reduce their anxiety level*. Children with auditory processing problems are often stressed and anxious in the classroom. This further inhibits their processing, and a negative cycle is formed. Sensitivity to these children's special needs and anxiety is a key factor in helping them to function effectively in the classroom. As the teacher grows to understand the students' styles and learning challenges, make sure the students are aware of these factors too, so that they can grow to become their own best advocates.

Visual Processing

Sam sits with a book held in front of him, concentration furrowing his brow.

"Can you tell me what you've read?" you ask.

Sam looks blank. "I can't remember," he says bleakly. "I have to hear it to remember it. I'm just no good at reading and spelling!"

Many children struggle with difficulties in *visual processing*. These children are often the opposites of children who have auditory problems. Areas that might be challenging for children with visual processing difficulties are:

♦ Remembering things they have seen

♦ Copying from chalkboards

♦ Reading aloud (and often the act of decoding)

♦ Visualizing scenes while reading

♦ Following maps

♦ Doing math problems (particularly geometry)

♦ Spelling

♦ Completing art projects and other visual activities

Children with visual processing problems often suffer in reading comprehension areas; however, with adequate language skills they can thrive in discussion and lecture settings (Levine, 1995). They are often highly verbal and rely on their auditory channels and memory to help them compensate. As in the case of auditory processing difficulties, these children usually have normal vision. It is in the *processing* of visual information with which they have difficulty.

What strategies can I use in the classroom?

There are many strategies a teacher can use to help these children in the classroom:

1. *Provide auditory reinforcement.* Often students who are weak visually rely heavily on their auditory-verbal skills. Therefore, providing adequate verbal reinforcement (such as discussions and lectures) is key for these students.

2. *Give specific academic help if needed.* Visual weaknesses often translate into serious academic difficulties in reading, writing, and language. A student may need specific academic help, such as tutoring, in these areas.

3. *Provide hands-on experience.* Many students benefit from taking a hands-on approach to learning. Novels and history can be brought to life with theater or puppets. Working in small groups with peers often can help students to supplement their weaknesses while providing their strengths to the group.

4. *Try alternative assessments.* As mentioned before, trying an alternative mode of assessment can realize a student's strengths. Oral presentations, "living histories," dioramas, pictures, and even composed music as a measure of student's knowledge of class material can provide a breadth of assessment that is critically important.

5. *Use computers.* Because visual weaknesses and writing issues often go hand in hand, the use of the computer is often a

Children with visual processing problems often suffer in reading comprehension areas; however, with adequate language skills they can thrive in discussion and lecture settings (Levine, 1995).

good tool for these students. This allows students to work at their own pace in composing and editing their written work.

6. *Give extra time.* Many students with visual weaknesses have retrieval issues: It takes them longer (and it is difficult for them) to retrieve information from memory. Often extra time is just what they need. This can be while taking tests or even while answering oral questions in class. Having extra time can allow them to access the information they need in an anxiety-free setting.

Organizational Skills

Alex has great ideas, however, she often cannot get started on projects. Once started, she finds it hard to work in a sequential fashion, and often starts in the middle, or writes the end of a story first. Alex continually loses things, and feels she can rely on her memory for assignments and information, as opposed to keeping a notebook. She often works slowly and needs extra time to get things to her liking. While Alex is intelligent and creative, she often does not complete projects or ends up doing them hurriedly at the last minute.

Alex portrays the typical child who suffers from *organizational issues*. These children have difficulty in the classroom and beyond in ordering their thoughts, their materials, and their day.

There are different types of organizational skills. One is the ability to organize materials. Children with difficulties in this area are untidy and often lose things. Their desks and rooms are usually quite messy. However, they often feel that they know exactly where an item can be found.

Another type of organizational skill is organization of time. Children with difficulty in this area cannot plan their time efficiently, such as planning for long-term assignments. They have difficulty estimating how long something will take to do and how to efficiently divide a task into workable pieces. Often these children also have a poor sense of time and do not realize if they have been working 5, 15, or 45 minutes on a task.

What patterns might I see in the classroom?

Because these children often lack a consistent, internal structure, they usually need one provided for them. Having a consistent schedule that is predictable can help tremendously. Anticipating weak moments, such as after lunch or transitions between classes, can help, too. Transitions can often produce anxiety for these children, causing them to "act out" or to forget needed materials.

Organizational skills are linked closely to perceptual organization, and children with weak organizational skills will often be weak in spatial skills as well (Levine, 1995). Orienting themselves using maps and finding their way from one place to another in a timely fashion may be particularly challenging for this type of child.

One particular subset of children with organizational issues is children who also have visual processing difficulties. These two difficulties can often be seen together as an area of weakness. Reading comprehension can be particularly difficult for them, as can mathematics and creative writing. Because both organization skills and visual processing skills can be linked to frontal lobe functioning (Luria, Karpov, & Yarbuss, 1966; Pennington, 1991), and because the frontal lobe continues to mature through adolescence (Bjorklund, 1995; Healy, 1990), these weaknesses can sometimes lessen or disappear as the child grows older.

What strategies can I use in the classroom?

There are several things a teacher can do to help minimize a student's organizational issues:

1. *Structure is key.* Most of these children cannot create a structure for themselves and thus need an external force (such as a teacher or parent) to create it for them. The goal is to teach children how to structure with organizers, schedules, charts, and lists, so that they can learn to organize themselves. Understandably, the more consistent the teacher is in her daily routine and expectations, the easier it will be for the disorganized child.

2. *Try to delineate the child's style.* Sometimes, what appears to be disorganization to an outsider is organization for the student; one of my students fondly referred to her desk as "the organized mess." Have the student explain how she organizes herself. Often disorganized students work horizontally (spread out items over space) rather than in the traditional vertical (making piles of like items). Try to find a balance between the student's natural proclivity and the needs and constraints of the classroom.

◆

The goal is to teach children how to structure with organizers, schedules, charts, and lists, so that they can learn to organize themselves.

◆

3. *Using a timer* can sometimes help a student who is having difficulty pacing herself or having difficulty gauging how long she is spending on a task.

4. *Set aside time each day to meet with the student before she goes home,* if at all possible. This will allow you to see if she has the correct homework assignments and the proper books and supplies that will be needed for doing them.

5. When assigning long-term projects, work with the student to build an appropriate work schedule. This will allow for the student to be able to complete the work in a timely, organized fashion.

6. Try to make transition periods smooth and not a time when you give out assignments or other important information. This will be to the benefit of many students.

Attention Deficits

Haley seems to be in constant motion. Whenever you look at him he is squirming in his seat and sometimes falling onto the floor. His work is messy. His presence can be like a whirlwind and he seems to have the unfortunate ability to unintentionally knock into things, such as other students. However, while sitting still appears to be a challenge (such as during a group listening activity), he can remain fixed and focused for an extended period while working on the computer, playing video games, or watching television. Haley seems to be a bit perplexed by himself, also, and your feeling is that many of the other children do not like to be around him.

Haley is a textbook example of a child with *attention deficit-hyperactivity disorder*. Commonly referred to as ADD or ADHD, attention deficits are being diagnosed much more commonly than they were 20 years ago, when names like "hyperkinesis" or even "minimal brain dysfunction" were applied to these children. To better understand the phenomena of attention, and thus the many students who are labeled as deficient in attentional skills, it is best to first step back and understand the theory behind attention deficit disorder.

What is an "attention deficit"?

Attention and arousal are two of our most basic, primitive abilities. For thousands of years, the capacity to attend has helped man to survive in an often hostile world. The attentional system is complex, multifaceted, and still not completely understood. For educators' purposes, a child with an attention deficit has difficulty in *sustaining attention* and/or in *inhibiting themselves*. This ability to sustain and inhibit is linked to neurotransmitters in the brain, chemicals that carry messages from one neuron to another, thus "carrying the message" to the body. If there are not enough of these transmitters, a breakdown occurs.

How is ADD/ADHD diagnosed?

In the United States, the diagnostic criteria for an attention deficit are defined by the *Diagnostic and Statistical Manual of Mental Disorders*, fourth edition (DSM-IV) (1994). Currently, all types of attention deficit are termed "ADHD" for clarification and facility. As the criteria indicate, it is through the "typing" of ADHD that information is given that delineates the nature of the deficit (inattention, hyperactivity/impulsivity, or both). (See Appendix A on pages 24–26 for ADHD criteria.)

What other therapies are there besides medication?

In addition to the more traditional classroom suggestions, there are two types of modification strategies that have been used with children with attention deficits.

One well-known method is *behavior modification*. This technique is based on the principles of classical conditioning: Positive actions earn positive reinforcement and negative actions are not rewarded. An individualized behavior modification program might focus on the child earning stickers for such behaviors as remembering not to speak out during math class or remembering to bring in his homework. At the accrual of 5 or 10 stickers, the child might earn a special privilege, such as being line leader for the day or getting to pass out papers. Behavior modification classrooms also can take the form of a "token economy," where students earn tokens for good behavior and can save them toward "purchasing" a reward at the end of the week. One of the basic tenets of behavior modification proponents is that *for the reward to be desirable, it should be something chosen (within reason) by the child*. This adds to the reward's value. The end goal of behavior modification is for the child to grow to be rewarded internally by these learned behaviors and to eventually not need material rewards in order to perform as desired.

◆

It is a goal of cognitive behavior therapy to have students learn to internally reward and support themselves in desired classroom behaviors.

◆

Another technique is known as *cognitive behavioral therapy*. This sometimes controversial technique focuses on a cognitive approach to instilling desired behaviors. The four main aspects of this technique are (1) identify the problem, (2) explore strategies, (3) review consequences, and (4) choose a strategy.

An example of cognitive behavior therapy is the example of Alexandra, an 11-year-old student with attentional issues who consistently forgot to put her name on her school papers. Different strategies were explored with her teacher, and the idea of writing an index card with a memory cue (*Did I put my name on my paper?*) taped onto her desk was decided. Alexandra felt that having this card on her desk would help her to remember, and eventually the card could move *into* her desk, and then hopefully not be needed any more. She selected this strategy, and was successful.

In addition, students are taught to reward themselves with internal self-rewarding statements, such as remembering to tell themselves "Good job!" when they have succeeded. Coping statements are another activity that allow students to bolster their confidence by telling themselves to "Keep trying!" Attention-focusing statements, such as "Now what do I need to remember to do?" at the start or end of lessons also are developed. These internal strategies are learned through role-playing with a teacher and are modeled by the teacher for the student. It is a goal of cognitive behavior therapy to have students learn to internally reward and support themselves in desired classroom behaviors. (I have found this technique easier to use and more successful with children age 10 or older.)

How does medication help?

In the United States, there are two major types of medications that are commonly prescribed to help students with attentional difficulties. One of these is the class of *stimulants*, such as Ritalin (also known as methylphenidate). Many people wonder: How can more stimulant help a child who appears over-stimulated to begin with? The theory behind this seeming paradox is that the additional medication provides a "jump-start" to an erratically working system. The additional stimulant provides for any possible deficiencies, and supplies enough synthetic neurotransmitter to swing the attentional control system back into proper working order.

The second major class of medications is *antidepressants*. These are often given to teenage students who also may be battling depression along with learning and attentional issues.

These medications block the absorption of neurotransmitters. Generally, neurotransmitters are released into the synapse between two neurons and any "left-over" neurotransmitter that was not needed to carry messages gets absorbed back into the system by a "vacuum" (Carlson, 1994). The role of antidepressants is to block the vacuum so that an abundance of neurotransmitters remains in the system. This is particularly key for the student who is suffering from a true *deficit* of transmitter.

A word about overdiagnosis

Many researchers and educators are concerned about what seems to be an overdiagnosis of children with attention deficits. Part of this concern stems from the fact that many of these children are diagnosed and then medicated for what seems at times a mysterious condition. There also is no clear, definitive answer as to exactly what ADHD is, or why it is. In fact, the diagnosis can seem somewhat "backward" when children are given trials of medication and, if they are successful, they are then diagnosed.

Educators should keep a few points in mind:

◆ Expect behavior alterations when children have been given behavior-altering drugs. Because a child performs better when medicated does not necessarily mean he has a chemical disorder. Changing the chemical balance in the brain can have behavioral changes in so-called "normal" children. It is important to ask, "Can the child cope without medication or is there a significant improvement only when he is being medicated?"

◆ Medication, while it is highly beneficial to those who truly need it, does not cure learning disabilities or raise reading levels. Students with a learning disorder in addition to ADHD will still need support in those areas.

Students who have lost classroom time due to inattention will probably need some remedial support, too. The benefit of medication is that it can make the child more teachable, though it can do nothing for subject matter that the child has missed.

◆ Medication can be hit or miss. It often takes some trials to get the correct dosage and timing. Teachers should be attuned to the child's moods, alertness or sleepiness, and hunger (or lack of), in order to provide important feedback to parents regarding the child's optimum dosage.

◆ If you see no difference in a medicated child, be sure to say just that. If a child is not responding to medication, he should not be on it. It is possible that the medication dosage is incorrect, the child is unresponsive to the type of medication given, or the child's problem is not a chemical one.

What about the student in class?

A student with an attention deficit can be exhausting to have in the classroom. Many of the strategies discussed for children with processing or organizational difficulties can be applied to ADHD children as well:

1. *Keep directions simple.* This will understandably facilitate comprehension.

2. *Gain eye contact.* This can be particularly helpful for ADHD children, as it allows them to focus on you before receiving information.

3. *Present information in a variety of modes.* Writing *and* saying directions and other information will reinforce comprehension.

4. *Give key points at the beginning and end of speaking.* This is helpful for both longer academic lectures and shorter "what we are going to do today" capsules.

5. *Allow for more review and reinforcement.* The more one-on-one time you can have with the student, the better.

6. *Allow more time for tests or the taking of untimed tests.* This can make a world of difference to a disabled student.

7. *Be consistent.* Consistency and structure are two important elements for optimum classroom functioning for children with attention problems.

8. *Try to keep distractions to a minimum.* This is often easier said than done, but important, nonetheless.

9. *Allow the student to tape record lectures to review later.* This will help to alleviate missing information.

Consistency and structure are two important elements for optimum classroom functioning for children with attention problems.

10. *Allow the student to take tests orally into a tape recorder.* This can help to facilitate the student's ability to "show what he knows."

11. *Have the student explain how he learns.* This can give you exceptional insights.

12. *Find the weaknesses.* Remember, ADHD is often accompanied by other learning disabilities. Be sure that these disabilities are also uncovered so that they can be remediated.

13. *Find the strengths.* Help students to realize and capitalize on what they do well inside or outside the classroom. This will help to reinforce self-esteem.

Written Output Difficulties

Jean sits at her desk and stares at a blank piece of paper—and stares and stares and stares. "I can't think of what to write!" she says plaintively. You suggest three or four ideas that fit the assignment and leave Jean to think about them. Ten minutes later you notice Jean staring out the window, her page still blank. When you approach her and ask her to describe something she might write about, she is able to tell you some ideas and narrate a lengthy event that would be fitting for the assignments. You suggest that she writes about what she just told you. "I can't. I don't know how," she replies forlornly.

Jean is a student who has difficulty in *written language output*. Her oral expression is fine: She is able to fluently relate events and tell her ideas. However, when asked to write her ideas, Jean encounters a stumbling block. She is apparently incapable of writing an adequate amount of material on paper, and the material she does write is produced through great effort and trial.

For many children like Jean, written assignments are a nightmare. These children are unable to produce the quantity or quality of work that is expected of them. For some reason, the mind/motor connection is not forged strongly, making this channel of output a weakness. Yet clearly they have good ideas, and many students, like Jean, can clearly express what they *want* to say, they just cannot write it down. Often once it is written, it is illegible or awkward, and the student is not happy with it.

How can a teacher help?

They are several things a teacher can do to help facilitate the writing process:

1. *Break down writing assignments into workable "chunks."* This will aid the student in organizing ideas for output.

2. *Talk out ideas first.* Sometimes a student will need to get her thoughts in order before sitting down to write. Remind her that good writers know where they are going and where they have been.

3. *Use a computer.* This technological tool can be extremely beneficial to those students with motor or spelling issues. Although students might be resistant at first because some will write faster than they can type, the computer will undoubtedly become an important writing aid as they grow older.

> ◆
>
> One of the most important things you can do for students with expressive language difficulty is to give them enough time.
>
> ◆

4. *Edit, edit, then edit again.* Though tedious, this can be where the best learning takes place, as students begin to realize what requires editing in their writing and how to edit.

5. *Encourage peer editing.* Not surprisingly, students are often resistant to suggestion from adults to change their writing. Their sense of ownership can sometimes be a bit extreme. Peers provide another audience that is generally receptive, yet still critical. In addition, all children should have the opportunity to give feedback.

6. *Make writing meaningful.* Children will find writing more enjoyable and easier to do when the topics are meaningful to them. Have students choose their topics and even the type of writing they will do. Conveying information about a place they visited, writing instructions or rules for a game for peers, listing classroom guidelines for the bulletin board, or creating stories for a class publication are some ideas of writing tasks that do not disappear when the pen is put down. As children begin to see the value in writing and in written communication, they will realize that writing goes far beyond the classroom.

7. *Focus on process, not product.* Many students are overly anxious about the appearance of their final product: how long, how neat, and how fancy it looks. In truth, although the final piece of writing is key, it is in the *process* that children learn the components of good communication. As teachers reward and focus on the steps to getting to the final product, students will begin to focus on these critical steps themselves, and be less concerned with how long their piece needs to be.

Are there other types of written output problems?

Other children, unlike Jean, have a more global form of expressive difficulty. Not only is writing difficult, but putting their thoughts and ideas into words is difficult. Some of these children have "word-finding problems," in which they cannot retrieve the word needed, though they clearly know what it is. This can be extremely frustrating and make writing (generally a more difficult task than talking) quite arduous.

One very important strategy

One of the most important things you can do for students with expressive language difficulty is to *give them enough time.* Retrieval and expression are difficult, but rarely impossible for them. They need time to process and formulate and to not feel pressured. Retrieval issues, like auditory issues, are compounded under stress. If a student feels pressured to perform and is having difficulty, she probably will have increased difficulty. Having an untimed or flexible time setting will help the student stay calm and work at her own pace, allowing her to work at her potential. In addition, children with extreme difficulty should be receiving individual help from a speech and language tutor or other support personnel.

Forming a Partnership With Parents

As teachers come to understand their students, they can facilitate other students' understanding of learning differences. These learning differences usually extend beyond the immediate classroom and can be seen at home as well. Teachers can enlist the help of parents, and also aid in parents' understanding of their child's learning. Because understanding a child's learning style goes beyond the classroom, parents can have important information to add as to their child's daily functioning and strengths and weaknesses. Additionally, some of the child's strengths may not be as evident inside the classroom as outside of it, and it is important for the teacher to be aware of these strengths in order to understand and appreciate all aspects of the child.

By working together, teachers and parents can create a consistent set of expectations for each child.

Frequent communication and team meetings, in which parents and teachers openly and directly communicate as to a child's progress and learning goals is essential. Involving specialists that work with the child, such as a reading specialist, physical therapist, or psychologist, is important as well.

By working together, teachers and parents can create a consistent set of expectations for each child and structure home and school environments in ways that will help the child be successful. In fact, the suggestions in this booklet are practical, easy-to-implement ideas that a parent or caregiver can use at home if he or she is working with a child. Having a predictable structure and routine to their learning and studying environments can only serve to help children as they grow to be independent learners. To achieve this, the children must be actively involved in their own learning and in understanding themselves. Thus, they can learn to be effective advocates for themselves, as they strive to attain the important, overall goal of being lifelong, active learners who are comfortable with their own strengths and weaknesses.

Conclusion

Children with learning differences can be a true challenge in the classroom. One of the first steps a teacher must undertake is to gain an accurate understanding of what the students' needs are. Specialists, such as school psychologists and learning disabilities specialists, can provide fundamental information that is critical for determining whether a child has a different learning style or a specific learning disability and how extensive the learning needs are.

Teachers must then keep these students' particular needs in mind while attending to the needs of *all* students. Often a deeper understanding of learning difficulties will lead to the creation of strategies and compensation that can help other children in the class as well, because each student is bringing his or her own unique set of strengths and weaknesses to the classroom. Each classroom can have a specific set of strategies for supporting weaknesses while celebrating strengths. With time and persistence, a classroom of differences can become a classroom of learners and a rewarding experience for all those involved.

Appendix A

Diagnostic Criteria for Attention-Deficit/ Hyperactivity Disorder

From American Psychiatric Association. (1994). *Diagnostic and Statistical Manual of Mental Disorders* (4th ed.). Washington, DC: Author.

A. Either (1) or (2)

(1) **Inattention:** At least six of the following symptoms of inattention have persisted for at least six months to a degree that is maladaptive and inconsistent with developmental level:

   a) often fails to give close attention to details or makes careless mistakes in schoolwork, work, or other activities

   b) often has difficulty sustaining attention in tasks or play activities

   c) often does not seem to listen when spoken to directly

   d) often does not follow through on instructions and fails to finish schoolwork, chores, or duties in the workplace (not due to oppositional behavior or failure to understand instructions)

   e) often has difficulties organizing tasks and activities

   f) often avoids, dislikes, or is reluctant to engage in tasks that require sustained mental effort (such as schoolwork or homework)

   g) often loses things necessary for tasks or activities (e.g., toys, school assignments, pencils, books, or tools)

   h) is often easily distracted by extraneous stimuli

i) is often forgetful in daily activities

(2) Hyperactivity-Impulsivity: At least six of the following symptoms of hyperactivity-impulsivity have persisted for at least six months to a degree that is maladaptive and inconsistent with developmental level:

Hyperactivity

a) often fidgets with hands or feet or squirms in seat

b) often leaves seat in classroom or in other situations in which remaining seated is expected

c) often runs about or climbs excessively in situations where it is inappropriate (in adolescents or adults, may be limited to subjective feelings of restlessness)

d) often has difficulty playing or engaging in leisure activities quietly

e) is often "on the go" or often acts as if "driven by a motor"

f) often talks excessively

Impulsivity

g) often blurts out answers before questions have been completed

h) often has difficulty awaiting turn

i) often interrupts or intrudes on others (e.g., butts into conversations or games)

B. Some symptoms that caused impairment were present before the age of seven.

C. Some impairment from the symptoms is present in two or more settings (e.g., at school and/or at home).

D. There must be clear evidence of clinically significant impairment in social, academic, or occupational functioning.

E. Does not occur exclusively during the course of a pervasive developmental disorder, schizophrenia, or other psychotic disorder, and is not better accounted for by another mental disorder (e.g., mood disorder, anxiety disorder, dissociative disorder, or personality disorder).

ADHD TYPING:

Attention-Deficit/Hyperactivity Disorder, Combined Type: if both criteria A(1) and A(2) are met for the past six months.

Attention-Deficit/Hyperactivity Disorder, Predominantly Inattentive Type: if criterion A(1) is met but not criterion A(2) for the past six months.

Attention Deficit/Hyperactivity Disorder, Predominantly Hyperactive-Impulsive Type: if criterion A(2) is met but not criterion A(1) for the past six months.

Attention Deficit/Hyperactivity Disorder Not Otherwise Specified: This category is for disorders with prominent symptoms of inattention or hyperactivity-impulsivity that do not meet criteria for Attention Deficit/Hyperactivity Disorder.

Appendix B

Suggested Readings

The following list of resources may prove useful for readers who would like to pursue the topics in this booklet further.

Cullinan, B. (1993). *Pen in hand: Children become writers.* Newark, DE: International Reading Association.

Fielding, E.N. (1993, June/July). Dealing with auditory processing problems in the classroom. *Reading Today,* p. 28.

Fielding, E.N. (1994, August/September). Reaching and teaching the ADD student. *Reading Today,* p. 27.

Fielding, E.N. (1994/1995, December/January). The case of the messy desk. *Reading Today,* p. 28.

Fielding, E.N. (1995, August/September). Teaching to the strengths. *Reading Today,* p. 29.

Fielding, E.N. (1995/1996, December/January). Making writing meaningful. *Reading Today,* p. 29.

Ornstein, R., Thompson, R., & Macaulay, D. (1984). *The amazing brain.* Boston, MA: Houghton Mifflin.

Rosner, J. (1989). *Helping children overcome learning difficulties: A step-by-step guide for parents and teachers.* New York: Walker.

Silver, L. (1984). *The misunderstood child: A guide for parents of learning disabled children.* New York: McGraw-Hill.

Silver, L. (1992). *Attention Deficit Hyperactivity Disorder: A clinical guide to diagnosis and treatment.* Washington, DC: American Psychiatric Press.

References

American Psychiatric Association. (1994). *Diagnostic and statistical manual of mental disorders* (4th ed.). Washington, DC: Author.

Bjorklund, D.F. (1995). *Children's thinking: Developmental function and individual differences.* Pacific Grove, CA: Brooks/Cole.

Carlson, N.R. (1994). *Physiology of behavior.* Boston, MA: Allyn & Bacon.

Healy, J. (1990). *Endangered minds: Why children don't think and what we can do about it.* New York: Touchstone Books.

Healy, J. (1994). *Your child's growing mind: A guide to learning and brain development from birth to adolescence.* New York: Doubleday.

Levine, M. (1995). *Educational care.* Cambridge, MA: Educators Publishing Service.

Luria, A.R., Karpov, B.A., & Yarbuss, A.L. (1966). Disturbances of active visual perception with lesions of the frontal lobes. *Cortex, 2*(2), 202–212.

Pennington, B.F. (1991). *Diagnosing learning disorders—A neuropsychological framework.* New York: Guilford.

Singer, B.D. (1991). Auditory processing disorders: Perspectives and suggestions. *The Gazette, 1*(4), 2–10.